ISADORA
DUNCAN

Mason Crest Publishers, Inc.
370 Reed Road, Broomall, Pennsylvania 19008
866-MCP-BOOK (toll free)

Illustrations copyright © 2000 Isabelle Forestier

Published in association with Grimm Press Ltd., Taiwan

1 3 5 7 9 8 6 4 2

Library of Congress Cataloging-in-
Publication Data:

on file at the Library of Congress.

ISBN 1-59084-144-1
ISBN 1-59084-133-6 (series)

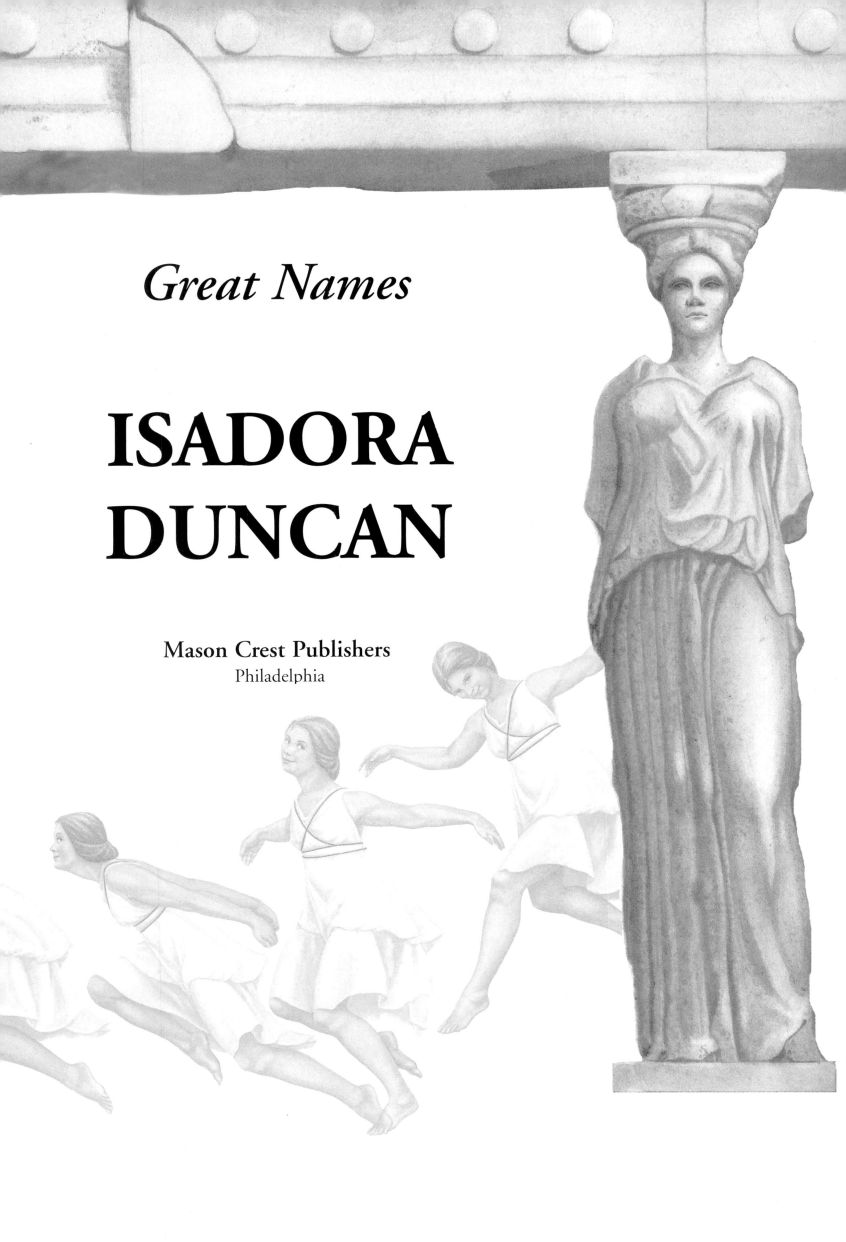

Great Names

ISADORA DUNCAN

Mason Crest Publishers
Philadelphia

When does a person's character begin to form? Isadora Duncan, the pioneer of modern dance, believed that a child's personality developed inside the mother's womb. Isadora's own personality seemed to exert itself before Isadora was born. When the future dancer's mother Dora was pregnant, she could only eat raw oysters and champagne. Dora declared: "This child is no ordinary human being."

Dora was right. The family's youngest child, Isadora, never stopped moving from the moment she was born. She began to dance as soon as she could stand. She would one day be called "Daughter of the Sun Spirit" and would attract the attention of the entire world. Isadora Duncan, born in 1877, would introduce a form of movement that would become the basis for modern dance.

Isadora did not like going to school. She viewed the public schools of the time as being cruel and controlling, much more than a person could stand.

Dora Duncan was a music teacher. Every day, she went to her various students' homes to give lessons. Dora did not have much time in which to discipline Isadora and her siblings. Isadora said: "When I was little, my family was very poor; but for me, that was a good thing. Because Mother couldn't employ governesses and servants, I was able to lead a carefree life in my childhood."

Each day when school ended, Isadora fled from her "prison" and ran off alone to play by the sea. On the seashore, Isadora used her imagination to her heart's content. In later years, Isadora looked back on those times and thought that the ocean waves had inspired her to create her special form of dance.

Isadora's real study time came in the evening. That was when her mother, who had been teaching all day, played the music of Beethoven or recited the poetry of Shakespeare and Shelley to her four children. And so Isadora's childhood was filled with music and poetry.

One day, Dora came home and found six little babies sitting on her floor. They were all too young to walk. In the middle of the tiny tots sat six-year-old Isadora, teaching the babies to wiggle their arms.

"What's going on? Whose children are these?" asked the astonished Dora.

"They are the neighbors' children," Isadora answered. "I am teaching them to dance. This is my dance school."

Dora was not angry at all. She sat down at the piano and began to play for the babies. The neighbors liked Isadora's dance school very much. They sent their children to study with Isadora.

Isadora's older brother Austin set up a theater in the barn. The Duncan children's performances became quite popular. Later, the entire family formed a theatrical troupe. They performed in towns and cities all along the California coast. At the time, Isadora was only twelve years old!

Isadora's dance performances grew more and more famous. One lady who came to a performance knew instantly that Isadora was very talented. Dora allowed the woman to take Isadora to San Francisco, where the young girl studied dance with a famous ballet teacher.

The teacher taught Isadora to stand on the points of her toes. Isadora asked why she should do so. The teacher answered that standing in such a way was very beautiful. Isadora answered: "In my opinion, this is a very ugly posture. It isn't natural." After only three lessons, Isadora refused ever to set foot in that classroom again.

Before Isadora Duncan became a dancer, the only recognized form of dance was ballet. In ballet, the dancers turned their legs outward from the hip, and used five basic standing positions. The dancers learned to do gravity-defying leaps. Ballerinas wore hard shoes and danced on the points of their feet.

Isadora hated ballet. She thought it was unnatural. She liked to let her body move in harmony with her spirit. She liked to run to the seashore and dance with the motion of the waves. She liked to dance along with the changing patterns of the clouds or to the feelings expressed by music and poetry. In her mind, that was what dance should truly be.

She still did not know that her way of thinking would stir up a revolution in the world of dance.

When is a family poor, and when is it rich?

Isadora's family lacked money, but they were rich beyond compare in their spiritual life. Sometimes, though, Isadora's mother would sigh: "Why is it that all four of my children are devoted to art, and not one of them is more practically inclined?"

In fact, Dora herself loved art and did not care much for material life. Not surprisingly, then, her children had little interest in wealth.

But poverty brings harsh realities, among them, the feeling of an empty belly. In the Duncan family, Isadora worked hardest to ease the effects of poverty.

When the family had no meat, Isadora would run to the butcher's shop and wheedle a piece of lamb from the butcher. When the family had no bread, Isadora would go to the bakery and persuade the owner to give her a loaf on credit.

In the Duncan family, Isadora took the initiative and became a leader. In later life, she took on a similar role in the world of dance, where she became an inspirational figure.

When Isadora was 16 years old, she performed solo in front of an audience, without any musical accompaniment. When the performance was over, someone in the audience called out: "You see, this was the Dance of Death and the Virgin." Isadora thought it should be called, "The Dance of Life and the Virgin." In Isadora's mind, the dance expressed her view of life, that behind all happiness lurked hidden grief.

When Isadora was 18, she decided that she and her mother would leave San Francisco, to try their luck in Chicago. But after they arrived in Chicago, Isadora could not find work. She and Dora sold everything they had that could be sold except one last thing of value: an Irish lace collar. She walked for hours under the hot sun, trying to sell the collar.

Finally, at sundown, she sold the lace. She used the money to buy a box of tomatoes. Isadora and her mother lived on those tomatoes for an entire week. They did not even have a slice of bread to add to their diet. Still, Isadora would not give up her dream of dancing.

In 1899, the Duncan family decided they would go to London, England. Isadora was 21 years old.

Before sailing to England, though, Isadora lost all her belongings in a fire. She was left with no money to pay for her boat fare. Isadora visited many wealthy society matrons, hoping they would sponsor her trip. They agreed to give her only small amounts of money.

In the end, the Duncan family decided to sail to London on board a ship carrying cattle. And so it was that this great

dancer and her family journeyed to London surrounded by several hundred head of cattle.

When the Duncans arrived in London, they had no friends and no money. They had no other choice but to sleep on the cold wooden benches in the park.

Nevertheless, the family enjoyed themselves in the great, historic city. Every day they visited Westminster Cathedral and the British Museum. They marveled constantly at all kinds of new things.

One evening, Isadora and her brother Raymond were dancing in a London park. A beautiful girl in a big black hat came walking by. Surprised at the sight of the two dancers, the girl asked: "Where are you from?" "We are not from any corner of the world," Isadora said. "We are from the moon."

The girl in the black hat was a famous actress. She introduced Isadora to many people. Gradually, Isadora had more and more opportunities to perform.

At first, people were not used to Isadora's style. But several artists were deeply moved by Isadora's dance from the spirit. Younger people especially liked Isadora's style. People who supported traditional ballet criticized Isadora. But her reputation grew.

She began to receive invitations to perform all over Europe. Because of her, people began to debate the meaning of dance.

Isadora's family always had been interested in the art of ancient Greece. After performing a number of times in public, the family traveled to Athens.

They arrived early one morning before the Temple of Athena. In the light of dawn, Isadora climbed up to the temple. She looked out over the beautiful landscape.

Her limbs began to tremble. Her heart was filled with adoration. She took in one long, deep breath and declared: "All that I know of life has been stripped from my body like a rough clothes. It seems as if I have never lived, and from this moment am truly born."

Isadora decided to abandon everything and settle in Athens. There she hoped to build the temple of her own ideal vision.

But there were problems. She had no land and no money. In the end, after staying for one year in Athens, Isadora had to give up this temple of her dreams.

Isadora returned to the dance stage. She put her ideas into more definite form, but still viewed ballet as unnatural. She commented: "Ballet training seems to be aimed at separating exercise of the body from that of the mind. That goes completely against my own ideas. I want to make the body a medium for the expression of the spirit."

Isadora sought the wellspring of the spirit. She wanted dance to reflect not the shadow of the mind but the shadow of the spirit.

When Isadora listened to music, she listened with her spirit. She became inspired. While the music played, Isadora raised her head, lifted her hands, and began to sway her body in dance. She loved to dance to the music of such great masters as Chopin, Beethoven, Schumann, and Wagner.

Isadora danced with bare feet and in filmy gowns that were nearly transparent. She believed that the body was pure and beautiful, and did not need to be covered from sight. In addition, she did not use stage sets.

From the time she was very young, Isadora liked to dance in front of a blue curtain. As an adult, whenever she performed, the backdrop on stage was always simply a sheet of pure blue.

Isadora set up her own dance school. Hundreds of parents brought their children to audition for admission. Isadora chose a group of students for the school. She dressed them like she dressed herself, in gowns that allowed the body to stretch and move freely.

Isadora did not charge any fees for tuition. She did not require students to study her dance steps. She wanted them to develop dances of their own spirit. She had them study art. She also taught them to observe the natural world, such as where the wind blew, how the trees swayed, and how the birds glided in the air.

Although Isadora was surrounded by many young students, her own three children were destined to leave her forever.

In the spring of 1913, Isadora's daughter Deirdre and her son Patrick went to lunch with their governess. On the way home, their car developed engine trouble. The driver got out to check the problem. Suddenly the car began to roll. It plunged into the River Seine. The two children and their governess drowned in the river.

In 1914, Isadora gave birth to another child. The baby died soon after birth. Isadora said: "I heard the sound of my own crying, but I had already lost consciousness. In a mother's life, there are only two occasions

when she will cry like this. Once when a child is born, and once when a child dies. When I held the infant's cold and lifeless hand in my own, my crying sounded exactly the same as it did when I gave birth. But one was inexpressible joy, the other inconsolable grief. Why can we not hear the difference between them?"

Stricken by these blows, the brokenhearted Isadora sank into a long period of depression. She could not dance at all. Whenever she saw someone else's child, it felt as if a dagger were piercing her heart.

Later, when Isadora and her family went to help refugees in Albania, they saw many unfortunate children. Isadora thought: "Although my children are dead, other people's children must face the terrible hardship of hunger and starvation. I can live to help them."

From then on, Isadora treated all children as if they were her own. Isadora returned to the stage. She gave performance after performance.

Most dancers give up dancing when they are still young; but Isadora did not stop. In 1927, when Isadora performed on stage in Paris, she was 50 years old. The audience never stopped cheering. She returned to the stage three times for curtain calls.

After the performance in Paris, Isadora and some friends set off for a holiday in Nice.

While the group was driving, Isadora's long scarf became entangled in a wheel from the car. Isadora was strangled to death. And so this dancer, who had always gone against tradition, met a tragic end to her colorful life.

During her life, Isadora drew artistic nourishment from art, music, literature, and sculpture. They provided the substance of her dance. Although she could not live to see how she inspired later generations, today there is not a single dancer who has not been influenced by her.

Whether in life or in dance, Isadora Duncan always went along her own path.

With her original style of dance, she danced her unique expression of life.